Crabapples

Pirates

Greg Nickles ❋ Bobbie Kalman ❋ Barbara Bedell

Crabtree Publishing Company

www.crabtreebooks.com

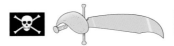 

Crabapples

created by Bobbie Kalman

To Sharon Swan, for her inspiration and love

Editor-in-Chief
Bobbie Kalman

Writing team
Greg Nickles
Bobbie Kalman

Managing editor
Lynda Hale

Editors
Niki Walker
Petrina Gentile

Computer design
Lynda Hale
Lucy DeFazio

Color separations and film
Dot 'n Line Image Inc.

Printer
Worzalla Publishing Company

Special thanks to
D.C. Smith and the Seattle Seafair Pirates; Benjamin "Blackbeard" Cherry and First Mate Dee Gee; Darvin Ebanks; Don Foster's (Subsea) Ltd. and the "pirates" of the *Jolly Roger*; all the other pirates who appear in this book; Michelle Mercure and the staff and students of the Montessori School of Cayman; Pat Bazell-Taylor and the Cayman Islands Pirates Week Festival Committee; Bloody Barney; David and Vicki Legge of Britannia Magazine; Collin and Matthew Owens; Brian Uzzell; Troy Kozma; and Barbara Leavy

Illustrations
All illustrations by Barbara Bedell except the following:
Lynda Hale: page 31; Janet Wilson: page 16; Winners of the Cayman Islands 1996 Pirates Week children's art contest: page 30

Reproductions
Howard Pyle, courtesy of the Delaware Art Museum:
"An Attack on a Galleon," detail, page 18; "Which Shall be Captain?," detail, gift of Dr. James Stillman, page 22; "Marooned," detail, Museum purchases, 1912, pages 24-25

Photographs
All photographs by Peter Crabtree and Bobbie Kalman except page 4, which is courtesy of the Cayman Islands Pirates Week Committee

 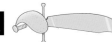 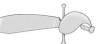 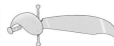

Crabtree Publishing Company

PMB 16A
350 Fifth Avenue
Suite 3308
New York
N.Y. 10118

612 Welland Avenue
St. Catharines
Ontario, Canada
L2M 5V6

73 Lime Walk
Headington
Oxford OX3 7AD
United Kingdom

Cataloging in Publication Data
Nickles, Greg, 1969-
    Pirates

(Crabapples)
Includes index.

ISBN 0-86505-633-1 (library bound)   ISBN 0-86505-733-8 (pbk.)
This book looks at pirates of the 1600s and 1700s. It presents information about ships, crews, clothing, flags, and life at sea, and suggests games and activities for children.

1. Pirates - Juvenile literature. I. Kalman, Bobbie. II.Title.
III. Series: Kalman, Bobbie. Crabapples.

G535.N54 1997   j910.4'5   LC 97-2240
                                                         CIP

What is in this book?

What is a pirate?

A pirate is someone who lives at sea and steals for a living. Pirates have sailed the seas for thousands of years, but the most famous ones lived in the 1600s and 1700s. They sailed their ships over the Atlantic and Indian Oceans and the Caribbean Sea.

Some pirates are famous for their scary names and fancy costumes. A few are well known because they stole huge treasures of gold, silver, or jewels. Others are remembered because they took prisoners and killed people.

It is wrong to rob and hurt people, and many pirates were punished for their crimes. Today, most people prefer to think of the fun things pirates did and the adventures they had. Some even pretend to be pirates by dressing up and playing games.

Famous pirates

There are many famous pirates. Some were **privateers**—pirates who worked for a king or queen. Most, however, were not loyal to any country and worked only for themselves. How many of these pirates do you know?

"Calico Jack" Rackham wore colorful cotton clothes. He married Anne Bonny.

Anne Bonny dressed as a man because women were not allowed to join ships' crews.

Legend has it that **William Kidd** buried a huge treasure.

Edward England let many of his prisoners go peacefully.

Dressed as a man, **Mary Read** fought alongside her friend, Anne Bonny.

"Black Bart" Roberts captured more than 400 ships!

Stede Bonnet was a wealthy man who became a pirate. He was captured by Blackbeard.

People thought **Blackbeard** looked like the devil. He wore red ribbons in his beard and smoking ropes in his hat!

At Nassau, Bahamas, **Charles Vane** crashed a fiery ship into the ships that were sent to catch him!

Parts of a ship

Pirates sailed the oceans in fast, well-armed ships, searching for towns and other ships to rob. A **galleon**, the largest ship, held about 300 pirates. Most pirates, however, sailed in smaller ships such as **sloops**, **schooners**, and **galleys**. Whatever its size, a ship had many different parts.

Masts hold up the sails.

sail

The crew lived in **quarters** below the deck.

The **rudder** turns a ship.

Cargo is stored inside a ship.

Sailors thought the **figurehead**, often a carving of a woman, calmed angry seas.

crow's nests

A **deck** is any floor of a ship.

figurehead

Gun ports opened so cannons could be fired from inside the ship.

The **hull** is the body of a ship.

Sailors could spot distant ships and land from the crow's nest.

Sails were controlled with ropes called **rigging**.

The pirate crew

Many pirates were needed to do jobs on the ship. Most crew members were sailors who hoped to make a lot of money. Some people joined a pirate crew to escape a harsh way of life. Others were captured by pirates and forced to work on the ship.

The ship's **surgeon** treated the injuries of the crew members.

The **captain** was elected by the crew and led only during battle. The rest of the time, the crew made the decisions.

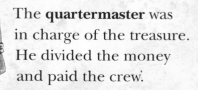

The **quartermaster** was in charge of the treasure. He divided the money and paid the crew.

There were many jobs besides those pictured here. The **sailing master** read maps and planned where to sail. The **gunner** was in charge of the ship's cannons. The **boatswain** kept track of supplies such as rum, water, food, and gunpowder. Members of the **regular crew** did odd jobs to keep the ship in good condition.

The **cook** made meals. Injured pirates often became cooks because they could not help sail the ship.

Musicians entertained the crew. During an attack, they made noise to scare their victims.

The ship's **carpenter** made all the repairs to the ship. If there was no surgeon, the carpenter sometimes amputated legs and arms!

Pirate clothes

Pirates wore clothes that made them look very different from other people. Some dressed in wild costumes to frighten their victims. A few wore fine, rich clothing. Most pirates, however, put together an outfit that would withstand weeks and months of rough weather at sea.

The picture below shows common pirate headgear. Pirates also wore baggy canvas pants or knee-length pants called **breeches**. Their boots or shoes had big, shiny buckles. Before an attack, pirates armed themselves with many swords and **pistols**.

feather

tricorne or three-cornered hat

hoop earring

eye patch

scarf

heavy coat

The "pirates" in the pictures above are dressed in traditional clothing. Their costumes include tricornes, bandannas, shiny jewelry, swords, and eye patches.

Pirate flags

All ships fly their country's flag. They also fly flags to send messages. Pirate ships used flags to identify themselves and scare other sailors.

The colors of pirate flags had different meanings. A black flag, such as the **Jolly Roger** above, meant death. A red flag meant that the pirates were out for blood!

A

B

C

D

Pirates decorated their flags with scary pictures. Match the meanings to the flags on this page, and you will avoid a grisly end! (Ha, ha, ha…)

1. A devil's smiling face means torture and disgrace!
2. Your troubles are about to start if you behold a bleeding heart.
3. Swords in a duel mean your end will be cruel.
4. An hourglass in flight will bring you endless night.
5. Bones that are crossed mean that lives will be lost!
6. A skeleton holds an hourglass to watch your final moments pass.
7. Death and dread follow this bony head.
8. The arm and a knife mean an end to your life.

Find out your destiny on page 31.

E

H

G

F

At sea

Life on a ship was hard. Pirates worried about storms, fires, falling overboard, and being injured during their long voyages. Many suffered from boredom, disease, and hunger.

There was little space or privacy in the crew's quarters. Spare ropes, sails, crates, and barrels were piled everywhere. At sea, the pirates had an unhealthy diet of salted meats, moldy biscuits, rum, and other foods that were stored on board for weeks.

Each pirate swore to follow a **code of conduct**, or set of rules. Pirates who broke the code got a whipping. Some disagreements were settled by a **duel**, a fight between two people using guns or swords.

Attack!

At sea, pirates spent most of their time hunting for ships to attack. Most victims surrendered, hoping the pirates would steal the cargo without hurting them. If they did not surrender, the pirates chased their ship. The pirates fired a **broadside**, cannon blasts and pistol shots that blew holes in the hull and sails and killed many people.

When their ship drew near, the pirates threw **grappling hooks** onto the other boat. These metal hooks were tied to ropes. The pirates pulled the boat closer and hopped aboard, swinging deadly swords and axes. Few people could win a fight against a bunch of fierce pirates.

Robbing and stealing

All pirates dreamt of capturing ships filled with gold, silver, and jewels. Most pirates, however, stole anything they could sell, such as tobacco and cotton. They also took tools, food, rope, and medicine, which they needed for themselves.

Many pirates took over ships that were carrying **slaves**. Slaves are people who are captured and forced to work without pay. Some slaves joined the pirates, but most were sold for money.

Maps were very valuable. Pirates stole maps to find towns to rob and safe harbors in which to hide. A few pirates may have buried treasure and drawn maps so they could find it later.

Maps were marked with symbols that had certain meanings. Use the symbols shown here to read this treasure map. Write a story about a pirate's treasure hunt on this island, describing the problems he or she had finding the reward.

—o-o-o-o— The treasure trail

✕ The spot where the trail begins

⚡ A deadly trap is nearby.

🗡 A dagger, knife, or sword points to the north.

◉ The treasure area

◯ A source of fresh water

5 The treasure is silver.

7 The treasure is gold.

222 Numbers that add up to six are bad luck. Is the treasure cursed?

Land ho!

When pirates needed to get supplies or repair their ship, they came ashore. On shore, the quartermaster sold the goods the pirates had stolen and divided money among the crew. Sometimes the pirates fought if they felt their share was unfair.

Pirate ships were **careened**, or cleaned, on a deserted beach. The crew hauled the ship on the sand and pulled it onto its side using ropes. The pirates then scraped the **barnacles** off the hull. Barnacles are small sea creatures with shells. The crew also replaced rotten wooden planks and sealed leaks with tar.

Pirates spent much of their time on land drinking and playing games. In a game called **mock trial**, pirates acted out a trial in a pretend court to make fun of the real courts that punished pirates. In the picture below, a pirate has been put in a **pillory** as a pretend punishment.

"Land ho!"

A pirate's fate

The careers of most pirates lasted only months or a couple of years. A few pirates grew rich enough to retire, but many were killed in battles or died from diseases. Some, like the pirate on the next page, were **marooned**, or left stranded on a deserted island. Pirates were marooned for committing a serious crime against their shipmates or for frequently breaking their ship's code of conduct. An abandoned pirate was left with only a pistol and a few supplies. Most marooned pirates starved to death.

Pirates were sometimes captured by pirate hunters. When a pirate was captured, he or she was taken to court to be tried. Judges often sentenced pirates to death by hanging.

To escape capture and punishment, many pirates turned themselves in and accepted a bargain called the **King's Pardon**. A pirate was pardoned if he or she promised to stop stealing. Some pardoned pirates became farmers or tradespeople. Others stopped stealing for a while but then went back to pirating.

Pirates of the islands

Many places, especially in the Caribbean, have histories that are full of pirate stories. Today, people in the Caribbean still remember the days when pirates sailed their waters and visited their shores. Some places hold special events to celebrate the fun and excitement of pirate life.

During the annual Pirates Week in the Cayman Islands, the residents and many visitors pretend to be pirates. They re-enact attacks, fights, and mock trials. A parade of colorful floats winds through the streets. Pirates Week also includes dances and displays of local history and traditional crafts such as rope-making and weaving.

The pirates at Pirates Week are not like those of the past. Some become pirates just for the fun of dressing up! They visit schools and warn students not to do drugs. Some entertain sick children in hospitals with pirate stories and songs.

Try these activities, matey!

Would you like to be a pirate and sail the seven seas? The activities on these pages will help you dress, talk, and even act like a pirate.

Look like a pirate

You can piece together an outfit from a few simple clothes, just as pirates did in the past. You need:

- a hat or bright scarf to wear on your head
- an eye patch
- a colorful shirt or t-shirt.
- a long scarf for a waist sash
- long stockings or pair of old jeans
- boots or plain shoes
- a long cardboard tube for a sword or spyglass.

1. Use the pictures in this book to help you dress up. You can be a neat, messy, fearsome, or funny-looking pirate.

2. Once you are dressed, create a pirate name that describes your personality.

3. Show off your costume to your friends. Ask them if they have seen any gold, silver, or jewels lately.

Aye, matey—pirate talk

Want to talk like a pirate? Here are some words and phrases to spice up your pirate speech:

landlubber A sailor's name for someone who has never been to sea

"Shiver me timbers!" An expression of surprise

buccaneer A kind of pirate that sailed the Caribbean in the 1600s

port A sailor's word for "left"

starboard A sailor's word for "right"

"Yo ho ho!" An expression used by jolly pirates

"Land ho!" "I see land!"

scurvy A disease caused by lack of vitamin C

"Weigh anchor!" "Haul up the anchor and set sail!"

merchantman A trading ship loaded with cargo

prize A captured ship

sea legs As soon as sailors were able to walk easily across the rolling deck and not get seasick, they had their "sea legs."

"Swab the deck!" "Mop the ship's deck!"

"About the leaks!" An order to fix the leaks in the hull

"Make him walk the plank!" Stories say that pirates forced people to walk down a plank and fall into the sea. Don't try this!

Fly a pirate flag

Making a pirate flag is easy. You need:

- a black or red rectangle of fabric or paper
- white fabric or paper
- a stick and some string
- scissors and white glue

1. Design a pirate flag using the symbols on page 15 or your own symbols.
2. Draw the symbols onto the white fabric or paper and cut them out.
3. Glue the cutouts onto the red or black piece of rectangular fabric or paper.
4. When the glue is dry, make two holes on one side of the flag and tie it to the stick with string. Your flag is ready for waving!

Picture some pirate art:

Use your paints, pencil crayons, crayons, or any other materials to make a piece of artwork about pirates. You could do a portrait or an ocean scene, or illustrate a story. Base your art on facts or make up your own subject.

A chest for your treasures:

Make a chest in which to store your treasures. You need:

- a shoe box with a removable lid
- wide, clear tape
- paints and brushes
- a water can for your brushes

1. Paint your shoe box and lid to look like a treasure chest.

2. Once the paint is dry, tape one edge of the lid to the box.

3. Fill your chest with treasures such as coins, stuffed toys, or other special objects. Remember to be a nice pirate—do not steal things to put in your chest!

Make a treasure map:

If you have secret treasure, you can hide it and make a treasure map. You need:

- a piece of yellow paper
- crayons, markers, or pencil crayons
- scissors

1. Hide your treasure. It could be hidden somewhere in your room, house, or yard.

2. On the piece of paper, draw a picture of the area where the treasure is hidden. Use the map and symbols on page 21 to mark where the treasure is located, in what direction to travel, and any dangers along the way.

4. Make your map look old and weathered by crinkling and folding it and snipping small bits from its edges.

Have a pirate party:

If you enjoy the activities in this book, you may want to have a pirate party. Invite your friends to dress up and play pirate with you. You could even host a pirate dinner, have a costume contest, or march in a pirate parade!

Answers to flag activity: 1-F, 2-H, 3-B, 4-E, 5-A, 6-D, 7-G, 8-C

Words to know

barnacle A small shellfish that attaches itself to underwater objects

broadside A blast from all the guns and cannons on one side of a ship

calico Brightly colored cotton fabric

careen To pull a ship onto its side in order to clean its hull

cargo The goods carried by a ship

code of conduct A set of rules that told pirates how they should behave

deserted Describing a place where no people live

duel A fight between two people armed with swords or pistols

figurehead A carving of a person, usually of wood, on the front of a ship

galleon A large ship, usually with three masts and square sails

galley A ship that uses oars to move

harbor A place where ships are sheltered from rough waves

maroon To leave someone on a deserted island

mock trial A game in which pirates pretended to be judges, lawyers, and prisoners in a courtroom

pardon To excuse a person's crimes

pillory A wooden frame with holes to hold a person's head and hands

pistol A gun that is held in one hand

privateer A pirate loyal to the king, queen, or government of a country

schooner A ship with triangular sails and two or more masts

sloop A sailboat with a single mast and two sails

Index

6 7 8 9 0 Printed in USA 6 5 4 3